You Don't Need 10

KATIE TAYLOR WYMAN

Copyright © 2025 Katie Taylor Wyman.

All rights reserved. No part of this book may be reproduced, stored, or transmitted by any means—whether auditory, graphic, mechanical, or electronic—without written permission of both publisher and author, except in the case of brief excerpts used in critical articles and reviews. Unauthorized reproduction of any part of this work is illegal and is punishable by law.

ISBN: 979-8-89419-539-1 (sc)
ISBN: 979-8-89419-540-7 (hc)
ISBN: 979-8-89419-541-4 (e)

Because of the dynamic nature of the Internet, any web addresses or links contained in this book may have changed since publication and may no longer be valid. The views expressed in this work are solely those of the author and do not necessarily reflect the views of the publisher, and the publisher hereby disclaims any responsibility for them.

Photo Credits:

Katie Taylor Wyman
Alesha Oster Photography
Amara Lea Photography
Erin Vournas Photography
Mary Catherine Anderson
TRP Studios

One Galleria Blvd., Suite 1900, Metairie, LA 70001
(504) 702-6708

Dear Reader,

I hope this book brings you peace, whether you are family, a friend, the parent of a limb-different child, the parent of a child with a noticeable difference or unnoticeable difference, or someone just looking for inspiration, I hope you're able to read this book and find comfort. We are all struggling with something in our lives, and we are all trying our very best. We are in this very small world together, and surely we can be kind to one another. We will make mistakes along the way, and we're all learning. Learning what is right, what worked, what didn't, and what God wants from us.

I also hope you understand my message that God graced us with Paisley to teach the world about acceptance and kindness, and therefore, it's okay to ask questions, and it is okay to be curious, but do so graciously. I think this whole journey is about educating people that being different is okay, it's not awful and it's not weird. Also understand it's hard and we will always struggle with this, but I am so grateful that God gave me this beautiful girl and honestly I wouldn't change a thing about her. She inspires me daily to be a better, braver person, and I couldn't be prouder of her. She's a gift from God, truly amazing.

God has a specific plan for each and every one of us, a plan he has had laid out since the beginning and a specific purpose for his plans.

Psalm 33:11 in the Bible says, "But the plans of the Lord stand firm forever, the purpose of his heart through all generations."

CHAPTER 1

Birthday

November 10, 2011, started out much the same as November 19, 2010. I had, after all, just been through this. I awoke to the alarm after a not-so-restful night. I was excited and nervous, my mind was racing, and I was terrified. After all this time, I knew exactly what could happen to you in a delivery room. I immediately went to the shower to get ready to meet my new baby—a girl this time. As I was showering, I was thinking of all the last minute things I needed to do before we left town, all the things that wouldn't get done, and I wondered if we were really ready to do this again. Oh well, I thought. Here she comes.

I hollered from the shower, "Honey, I think I'm going to change her name."

"What?" Russell said. "She isn't going to be Paisley?"

"No, she'll still be Paisley, but instead of Harmony Kay, I think she should be Taylor Kay. I need some tie to my family, and I loved my maiden name."

"Ok," he said. "Whatever you want is fine with me."

I got out of the shower and tried to do as many things as I could think of, and we were out the door.

In the car, I felt a little different than last time, but last time I was already in labor as I headed to the hospital. This time I wasn't sure, and we'd had so much trouble with this little spitfire already. She'd been refusing to be head down. We'd checked in a couple weeks earlier to turn her, and after the paperwork was filled out (just in case she happened to be born in the process), the doctor was ready to turn her, but the little lady had moved on her own. Well that was a waste! At least my paperwork is done, I thought, as we continued the drive to Sidney.

We arrived at the hospital, checked in, and were given the same room I had been in almost a year before; everything seemed to be moving right along. Please, God, I prayed to myself, don't let it take as long as last time. Thirty-eight hours in labor was not on my agenda again, but she was the second one, so hopefully it would be easier.

They started Pitocin almost immediately, and things were really getting under way. By about eleven fifteen that morning, I was ready for the epidural. As one nurse went to find the anesthesiologist, another checked for the baby's head. Shortly thereafter, my water broke, and the baby managed to move. She was no longer head down, and since my water had broken, there was nothing they could do. I was headed for a C-section immediately. I was hysterical, inconsolable, one of my worst fears realized. A C-section was the last thing I wanted. I realized that it was a serious situation and that it was the safest option for us at the time, but it was not my plan, and I was a mess.

Immediately, I was wheeled down and prepped for the procedure. It all happened so very fast. In a matter of minutes, they were cutting me open, and the doctor announced that she was now breech. She had managed to move again in the transfer from delivery to the surgical room. Then we heard her cry. I was still crying—cried through the entire thing.

While I was getting stitched back up they showed her to me. I didn't get to hold her, but they had her wrapped up in the typical hospital blanket, and she was beautiful, a tiny hand was sticking out of the blanket. I was an emotional disaster, still crying, but it was bittersweet. I had calmed down, wasn't so hysterical, and was so relieved that we were all ok. My husband by my side, baby girl had arrived to make a family of four. Russell left with Paisley and the baby nurse. A surgical nurse took over holding my hand, and I was put back together, stitched up, and sent to recovery. I slept for a while, which I needed after such an emotional morning. I'm sure they decided to medicate me so I'd sleep for a while, considering the condition I'd been in, and they knew I was going to receive more news when I woke.

When I awoke I was taken to my room. I was no longer in the large, comfortable delivery room but in a tiny, dreary room. I hadn't been able to deliver in the spacious, updated delivery room, so I'd had to move out. Russell was there, but the baby wasn't. He seemed anxious.

He looked at me, and with every ounce of courage and bravery he had, he said, "Paisley only has one hand."

I had just awoken from recovery, so I was a little foggy. "What?"

"She's missing her right hand," he said.

I looked at him and said, "Are you kidding? That's not funny."

"I'm not kidding, honey. There's a doctor waiting outside to talk to us."

I immediately broke down. "What do you mean, she only has one hand?" How, as a mother, did I not know that? I had just seen her. I realized they only let me see her a few seconds, and I didn't even get to touch her, and now that I thought about it, I remembered she was wrapped in a blanket, and only one little hand was sticking out, and then she and Russell were gone. How did this happen? Why did this happen? How does a baby not have 10 fingers and 10 toes?

"Where is she? I need her now!" I said.

The baby doctor that had been on call was no longer waiting in the hall to explain things to me. I guess when Russell informed him that he would be talking to his wife in private first, he split. I'm sure he had an emergency or something, but nothing was ever explained to me. I never did speak to him or anyone. No one ever tried to explain why my perfect beautiful baby only had one hand.

Russell went to the nursery and found our sleeping babe and brought her to me. She was so beautiful—the most amazing eyes and little doll face. We were both crying, soaking her in. How were we ever going to explain this to her? What were we going to do? How would we begin to explain this to anyone? We just sat for a while, the three of us.

Eventually we snapped back to reality and started to make a plan, we had phone calls to make. I really can't remember who called who or who I even spoke to that day, but my parents were on the list, as well as Monica (Russell's sister) and my dear friend Kelsey, who were all out of town. Chelsea and Sam, two of my coworkers that had become very close, almost family, were also informed. I don't remember any of the conversations, but I know they were hard. Russell's parents came later that evening and brought Jeten to meet his sister. He wasn't too interested in her. He just wanted his mom for a bit. Russell and his dad stepped out to eat. He hadn't eaten all day. Pam, Russ's mom, stayed with me. I wasn't feeling well at all. I was very uncomfortable and nauseated. I started vomiting and just really wanted to be alone. I wasn't feeling up to visitors or socializing. So much on my mind. I really wished Russ would hurry back. I told myself everything would work out. We could do this. We were strong. But, seriously, how was this happening?

We may not understand God's plan now…
But eventually we will. He is the author of our life.
Everything happens for a reason.

—Anonymous

CHAPTER 2

Hospital

The next day, my parents came to visit. They now had Jeten, so he was along and snuggled in bed with me. He could have cared less about his sister. He was too young to have a clue what was going on. He wasn't even one yet. We had a nice visit with them. My parents were unable to make it right when the baby was born, as they were out of town. But as soon as they got home, they came, and it was so nice to have my mom near. No matter how old you are, you still need your mom, especially in times like these. There were so many emotions at that time, and I think we were all relieved to be in the same room together.

There were lots of wonderful visitors over the next few days: my grandparents, Russell's grandma Pat, cousin Tara and baby Ryen, Russell's sister Lynn, Aunt Loretta, Aunt Judy, and Rick came back. Russell has a very large supportive family, and it was so nice to have them. I'm not from a large family, but I'd grown to consider his my own, and it was nice to have the support.

I'm sure the list of visitors is longer, but one specific visit sticks with me. Some friends of ours came to visit, Russell met them in the hall and walked them in. As they entered, I said to Russell, "Did you tell them about the baby?"

Paisley was not in the room, and immediately the wife was panic-stricken.

Russell said, "No, I didn't."

Everyone looked at me, and I said, "Paisley was born without her right hand."

The wife was instantly relieved. She had thought our baby hadn't made it.

They were so wonderful to have made the drive over from Williston to visit us. I was so thankful for their support as well. I realized from then on that I was going to do everything in my power to be the one to tell people about my baby before they saw her. I decided that it was important for me to say it upfront, before I had to see the looks of shock on faces. There would still be looks as I explained it, but this way it wouldn't happen while they were looking at her. Even in the hospital, no matter who was anywhere near her—nurse, visitor, or passerby—my immediate thoughts were, I wonder what they're thinking right now about my baby?

I remember her first bath, and I remember Jeten's. His took place in the nursery, and Russell's mother and two sisters witnessed it, and Monica took the most amazing photographs of the event. During Paisley's, it was just Russell, Paisley, a nurse, and I in our tiny hospital room. I remember holding her and looking down on her, wondering exactly what I should do with her arm, and wondering what feeling she had. I wondered what the nurse was thinking. Was she feeling pity for us? She never said a word about her, and she was so gracious during that intimate time. I was so very excited to get out of the hospital after three days and get this baby home, where we could protect her from people and choose how to introduce her to the world. We were going to be creating a safe place for her.

"The bible never once says, 'figure it out,'
but over and over it says, 'have faith.'
God already has it all figured out for us."

—Dave Willis

CHAPTER 3

Home

The night we arrived home with Paisley, my mom brought over dinner and tons of presents. My grandparents were in attendance and my brother. Paisley was able to attend her first "family dinner," something we do with my parents, grandparents, and brother weekly. It was so nice to introduce her to that family tradition. We took the first of many four-generation pictures with my grandma, my mom, Miss Paisley, and me.

Our first few days at home were rough. I wasn't handling the C-section very well. It was so very hard not to be able to do so many things I had before. After Jet was born, I was back to work almost immediately, and this time that wasn't going to happen. I had just lost my daycare two weeks earlier, and in this town at the time, we were booming, and daycare was scarce. I started a spreadsheet with lines and lines of data, trying to find someone to watch my babies. Since I was unable to care for Jet, my husband, Russell, was also stuck at home. We were all at home—one big happy family. Everyone was frustrated. Jet desperately wanted to be back playing with friends at daycare. A week or so later, I found a lady that was willing to take Jet starting December 5, so we had an end in sight. We had a few visitors while we were settling in at home, but not nearly as many as when Jeten was born.

I remember thinking, Doesn't anyone want to meet our precious girl? Is it because they don't know how to act around us? Don't know what to say?

When Jet was born, lots of people sent flowers. This time that was not the case.

I do remember a lunch date with a friend that came to meet Paisley. I remember her coming in, and the first thing she said was, "Well, I heard you had a little surprise when she was born."

Hmm, yes, definitely not what we were expecting. I think even at this point, several days later, we were still in shock. You have this preconceived notion that when you're having a baby, the baby will be born with ten fingers and ten toes. Never in my wildest dreams could I have imagined that this was going to happen to us. I still couldn't grasp how in this day and age we did not know. We had numerous ultrasounds with Jeten but not with Paisley.

I did opt for an ultrasound late in the pregnancy that was nonmedical, an optional one that we paid for and that both of our mothers came to. I remembered that we had a DVD copy from that day. I was curious as to what I might see there, so shortly after she was born, we were home alone, and she was sleeping, so I put the DVD in, and sure enough, there she was. I could clearly see, and I cried. I mourned her hand, but in that moment I decided we were going to do everything we could for this baby, give her every opportunity we could, and do everything in our power to give her normalcy and treat her the same way we did Jeten. We weren't going to let her use this as a crutch in life, and we were not going to use it ourselves. Our home was going to be her safe place, but out in that world, she was going to need to be brave.

May home be blessed with the laughter of children,
the warmth of a family, hope for the future,
and fond memories of the past.

—Anonymous

CHAPTER 4

Family Events

We like to entertain and have people over regularly, whether it's something really casual, like having another family over for a visit, or a big to-do, like a birthday. Birthdays are very important at our house and celebrated large! We haven't changed much of our entertaining style since Paisley was born, but we do our best to not invite anyone that doesn't know her, because it's important to all of us that the house be her safe haven. Jeten's first birthday was chaotic, to say the least. Paisley was nine days old, and it was an excuse for family and friends to see her, in addition to celebrating Jeten. Everyone that was there was either family or close friends, so there was no issue, but what I hadn't anticipated was our friends' children, but I handled that really well. I think it was so crazy around the house, and I was a mess of hormones, but that day was magical regardless. We had several of Russell's family members come from the nearby area, which was so great. Russ's aunt and uncle brought his grandma which we would always remember, as it was the last time she was in our home before she passed. I do remember one specific thing from the evening. I was passing through the living room, and a friend was holding P. One of his sons made a comment that I don't quite remember, but the response from the father was perfection: "That's just the way God made her." I smiled and continued on through. From the very beginning, and still today, that is my response to people's initial questions. It's the truth. God perfectly made her the way he wanted to, and we're blessed to be able to help show the world that everyone is made different in their own way.

A woman I have confided in, said to me once that she tells her son, "Everybody has something, even if you can't see it." That is so very true. Everyone in this world is dealing with something. Some we can see, and some we cannot. It truly is important that we remember acceptance and that we remember to educate our children so they understand that it really is ok to be different, and everyone is different in some way.

A close friend of mine replayed for me an experience with her daughter meeting Paisley for the first time. I'm not exactly sure when this took place, but it was in our home. They had come for a visit and brought their children. The younger ones don't remember meeting Paisley for the first time, as they were so young that that's how they've always known her, but their oldest daughter was old enough to see something different. I don't remember the event, because I didn't witness the parental exchange, but apparently she asked her mom about Paisley, and the mother quietly replied something like this: "That's how God made her, and we can discuss it further at home." The daughter, being the gracious mature child she was, accepted that answer from her mother, and that was the end of it.

To me that spoke volumes about the parenting style. That's how it should be, without a huge scene. I'm not saying that asking questions in public is wrong, but when the answer is "That's just the way God made her," that should be enough of an answer, and if the child wants to carry it further, they can with their parent in private. It's all about parenting and showing respect to the family involved. In this particular case, it showed us respect by not making a scene about our baby.

I had a conversation a couple years ago with Monica about how Annabel, Paisley's cousin, has never asked about Paisley. They see each other often, are only about seven months apart, and are the very best of friends. I think in that case it's the only way she knows Paisley. Most who have known Paisley since birth have never asked about her to my knowledge. It's just how they know her. It's who she is, and she's accepted.

When times are tough, we need to remember 2 Corinthians 5:7: "For we live by faith, not by sight." If we can hold steadfast in our faith, we will have hope.

CHAPTER 5

Daycare

We went to meet with the new daycare lady the first of December—a cold evening—and we brought Paisley with us. The lady seemed ok. She was nice enough, appeared to love children, and wanted us to know she was very religious. I started filling out the contract and making small talk. Jet was playing with toys and looking around. Paisley started to fuss, so I brought her out of the car seat carrier, and the woman became so excited. She said she would definitely be finding room for this baby in the near future because she loved special babies. Special babies? I guess because she was missing a hand she was special in her eyes. In my eyes she was special for so many reasons. I felt uneasy about the comments, but also felt that she meant well. I finished filling out the paperwork, and Jet started there December 5.

Paisley was able to go one day a week until there was a permanent spot, which was expected to be sometime in February. Thankfully I was blessed to be able to work from home; however, when Jet started daycare again, I decided I could go back to work in the office some. Paisley was a pretty quiet baby in the early weeks, and I figured it would be good for us to get out some. She ended up also getting into another daycare part time. All of the daycare experience and the exposure out of the house meant many, many questions about her, mostly from children, but it was a hard time to still be trying to process it and then have to answer questions too. At that time, I just so desperately wanted to have what I thought was a "normal" baby. Little did I know that there would come a time when I would think completely differently.

"People will forget what you said, people will forget what you did, but people will never forget how you made them feel."

—Maya Angelou

CHAPTER 6

Office

I had been in touch with Chelsea, Sam, and Alissa (the wonderful ladies I was working with and my dear friends) almost from the minute Paisley was born, so I was still in the loop on all the projects and gossip, and I especially wanted to hear every detail that was said about me and the rumors about Paisley. There were people that had come to the loft to ask them if it was true. The first day we came in, some of the other women in the office came upstairs to see us, and I specifically remember two women coming up to me, and before I took her out of the carrier, I said to them, "Have you heard anything about her?"

They both just looked at me and said, "No."

I said, "Well, she was born with only one hand. I like people to know that before they see her."

Tears welled in their eyes and I immediately felt for them. I wasn't trying to make them feel bad; I just really wanted them to know. Later that same day I reflected on the episode, and I wondered what I could have done differently. Should I have said that? Did I really need to tell people, or would it be better to just keep quiet and let them see her?

In the end, it was a case-by-case situation. There were times I felt it was important for people to know, and at other times it was a nonissue.

During the summers, we usually have at least one office barbecue, where we all get together with our spouses and children. Typically it is one of the only times I see my coworkers' children and vice versa. During one of the first events Paisley attended, I didn't witness this, but a coworker told me at a later date—apparently the coworker's little girl noticed Paisley's arm and asked him if she was ok. Her father said, "Yes, she's ok."

The little girl said, "And we love her?"

"Yes," said the father. "We love her."

"Oh good!" said the girl.

Those are the moments that melt my heart—when children see my daughter and, without a scene, have the grace to ask their parents about her and the love to accept her. I love hearing those stories from people.

Dear God,

Please continue to help me to do what you want with this beautiful soul you entrusted to me, help me to help her, and help the world in the process to accept her. I know you will help me in your own time and I will be patient in life in the meantime.

Amen.

CHAPTER 7

Ten Months: Shriners

From the moment Paisley was born, we were never told what her specific diagnosis was. A few people had mentioned amniotic band syndrome but no one we credited, and we weren't exactly sure how many bones she had past her wrist, if any. We had so many questions, and we wanted to know as much as we could to provide her the best options. Shortly after she was born, I was in contact with a surgeon in New York that specialized in very young children. He looked over her case and even presented it in a colleague forum, but no one ever felt that they had any surgical options for her. At her six-month checkup, we talked about some more options, and our pediatrician at the time recommended that we go to Shriners, in Minneapolis, so she could be evaluated and we could maybe learn some options. September 26, 2012, we made our way to my aunt and uncle's home in Alexandria, Minnesota. We had a wonderful evening together visiting, and my Aunt Susan made a wonderful pan of lasagna for us. Thursday, September 27, 2012, we awoke early and hit the road for the remaining trek into Minneapolis. We arrived at Shriners, checked in quickly, and sat in the waiting room. We didn't wait too long before they called our name. We gathered all of our belongings and started the extensive evaluation. They checked her over thoroughly, asked lots of questions, and looked over her medical file. We met with several people, including the doctor in charge of her case at the time. To be seen at Shriners you must be referred to a doctor, and we were referred to a surgeon in the beginning. He came in to meet with us and wanted to know what kind of surgery we were looking to do. Russell and I looked at each other and said we weren't looking for a surgery, just some answers and options for her future. He decided to take some X-rays to be sure of her situation but didn't think there was any surgery that was going to help her at that time. He did, however, refer us to the prosthetic department, which we were happy about, and honestly, it was what we wanted out of the visit. We knew nothing about prosthetics and wanted to know more about the options available.

After the pleasantries and getting shown around the department, the tech asked us what we were looking for and what she was struggling with. Well, we couldn't come up with anything. She wasn't struggling with anything. He made the comment that maybe when she started to ride her bike or play a sport, she might want a tool. He explained many situations where a tool might be necessary or appropriate and suggested we give him a call the instant we saw her struggling with something, and then he would whip something up to send us.

We had a wonderful appointment and truly learned a lot. They were so amazing to us, and for the first time since she was born, we had some answers. This was not amniotic band syndrome; this was simply a fluke. So many amazing things need to happen at just the exact right moment in the womb, and for some reason, at the moment her right hand was supposed to develop, it just didn't blossom and open up. We're so thankful every day for the arm she does have. She has a wrist where her right hand would have developed, which is so amazing for her. She has five little nubs at the end of the teeny fist that should have been a hand. One of the nubs has been known to grow a nail. She's also able to move it and occasionally find a use for it. In that little moment of creation, so many things could have happened differently. It could have been so much worse. We are so very blessed.

"I have told you these things, so that in me you may have peace. In this world you will have trouble. But take heart! I have overcome the world."

—John 16:33

CHAPTER 8

Eighteen-Month Checkup

I've always been great at getting the kids to their recommended checkups and have always been so proud of their milestones. For Paisley's eighteen-month checkup, it was just her and me. Usually the kids have them together, since they're so close in age, but Jeten didn't need one that month, so it was just us girls that day. The appointment went well. We didn't have to wait too long, and she was so happy that day. I love that age. They're so curious, are starting to verbalize more, know what they want, and move so well. I was so happy with her that day that I was glowing. She was walking so well, and she was proud too.

We left the room after her checkup, and I let her walk the halls of the clinic as we made our way out. We were not in a hurry, and I was enjoying watching her walk. As we came around a corner, we met another family on their way out: a father, a mother, and a child. It was an older child. I can't remember if it was a boy or girl, but I remember that I smiled at them and they smiled at us. Then all of a sudden, the father must have looked closer at her. He stopped in his tracts and said, "Oh, my gosh. What happened to her? Oh, that is so sad!"

I started to feel strange. "That's just the way she was born," I said. I picked up my baby and we fled the scene. I realized then that it was a mama bear situation. She didn't need to hear that. I didn't need that. We had been having such a wonderful moment, and then out of nowhere he had to say something. I'm all for curiosity or questions—to a point. But I'm a firm believer in the idea that it's not what you say but how you say it. I still look back on that incident in particular and think, Really? That's what you should say to the mother of that "poor child?" She doesn't need your pity, sir. I wish you could see her now, really see her in action. She is a master of living. There is absolutely nothing she can't do. She knows no difference, and you would be amazed.

I also think, Even if something had "happened" to her, why on earth would you think that would be your business? We don't know you, and I'm sure you could have found a better way to approach us.

Sometimes I also think (even though I know that I shouldn't, because God made her to teach the world to be more accepting), we don't owe you anything. You don't need any explanation or deserve answers.

For the most part, we do just fine in public and ignore most of what is going on, but it's moments like that that will stick with me. This was one of those situations, as I mentioned before, where we struggle. I know she was meant to lead the world into acceptance and understanding, but sometimes it's very hard on all of us. I also don't think that at that point I fully understood God's plan and was ready to take on the job of teaching acceptance. I just wanted to be happy with my baby and not be bothered. I've come a long way since that day.

"Do not be anxious about anything, but in every situation, by prayer and petition, with thanksgiving, present your requests to God. And the peace of God, which transcends all understanding, will guard your hearts and your mindsin Christ Jesus."

—Philippians 4:6–7

CHAPTER 9

Dance Class

As soon as I found out I was having a little girl, I began dreaming of tutus, frilly dresses, and a daughter in dance class. In 2014 I was desperate to find activities for my children to be in. I called around to several places offering gymnastics, swim lessons, hockey, and dance. We did gymnastics until they cancelled the 5:30 class we were in. The swim lesson times have never worked for us. Jet did try hockey that year, and I was able to get Paisley into what was then called baby dance. We joined the class after the season started, so her first day wasn't the same as everyone else's. When we arrived, we signed the paperwork and ordered the recommended items. As the class was about to begin, P clung to me like she sometimes does in a new environment, and there were girls and parents everywhere, since one class was ending and a new one beginning. Because it was her first day, I asked the instructor (a young girl of maybe fifteen or sixteen) if I could sit in, and she obliged.

We entered the room, and I sat in a corner on the floor as the girls lined up in the room. Paisley seemed so happy to be there and really excited about this. She was nervous and came over to me a couple times, but there was nothing that made me think she didn't want to be there. I noticed several of the girls staring at her and talking about her. I realized that a few of them had to be close to five or six, probably in kindergarten, and Paisley was just three. One girl in particular came up to Paisley a couple times and asked her why she was missing a hand and even touched her arm. I immediately wanted to leap from the corner to run interference but felt that I needed to let her work this out. This was one of her first experiences in a class setting, and she needed to figure it out.

They started learning their routine for the show they would perform in January. The theme was *Frozen*, which is one of Paisley's favorite movies, so she really seemed to enjoy dancing to that. She had a little trouble listening to her instructor and ignoring me, but I felt the first night went really well. It was both good and bad that I had sat in the room, but I thought it was ok for the first day. We left that night and she said she enjoyed it and wanted to go back next week.

Week two came, and she seemed excited to go back to dance. We arrived, and this time I told her I was going to sit in the waiting room with all of the other mothers. She hesitated and was nervous but agreed. She went in, the instructor closed the door, and I felt really good, so proud of her. Partway through the class, she came out and said she needed to go to the bathroom. I took her, and afterwards I sent her back into the classroom through the door by the bathrooms. I then stayed in the hallway and peeked in on the class to see how it was really going. From where I was standing, none of the girls could see me, only the instructor. I once again saw the same girl asking questions about Paisley's arm. I tried to tell myself it was just day two and that the newness would wear off. I did think, though, that they'd already been there close to a half hour. I wondered if she'd asked other questions that day. I tried to shake it off and not worry about it.

We left that night, and P said she enjoyed it and really liked dance class. When week three came around, we were getting ready to leave the house, and Paisley said she didn't want to go this week. I asked her why, and she said, "I don't want anyone to see me."

I thought it was a strange response and didn't quite understand the meaning at the time. I convinced her to go that night and go into the classroom with the instructor without me. That night, from what I could tell, seemed to go without a hitch; however, in the lobby, with the door closed, the mothers can't see a thing. We went home that night, and I didn't hear much about it.

Week four, we were headed out the door, and once again she said she didn't want to go. I again convinced her to go, and she asked if I would sit in the room. I told her I couldn't, that I had to sit with the other moms. We went back and forth several times, and I eventually gave in to her and sat in the room, but I told her she needed to listen to the teacher and pretend I wasn't there unless she really needed something. She agreed.

I sat in the back corner this time. I could see about the same, but I was by the door, so I thought maybe I could escape. Class started and seemed to be going fine. Then they were told to get in a circle. They had an activity to do. It was very similar to ring around the rosy, if that helps you to visualize it. The same little girl that had been asking questions for weeks and talking about P ended up next to her. She started to reach for Paisley's hand. But she pulled back and said, "Oh, I can't stand next to you. You don't have a hand." And off she pranced to the other side of the group.

Immediately, an instructor jumped in (they had two that day) and closed the circle, and they went on with the activity. I didn't move a muscle, didn't say a thing. My head was spinning. This was why she didn't want to come here. I felt this was never going to stop.

Looking back on that moment and looking forward, I'm not naïve. I know this is going to be a part of Paisley's entire life, but man, sometimes it can feel so out of control.

We left dance that particular night, and I didn't even know how to handle the situation, I didn't ask her how it went or if she wanted to go back. We talked about other things in the car and went home and read books and followed the normal bedtime routine.

The next day, I thought, What am I going to do about this? Do I let her quit? Do I make her go and use this as a learning experience? Dear God, please help me. What am I supposed to do?

The next morning, I decided to call the owner of the company and see what she thought. I also wanted to know if there was another class Paisley could go to. We talked for a while about it, and she suggested to me that maybe the next time I could come into the classroom and try to talk to the girls about Paisley and answer any questions. I could tell them she was fine and see if by talking to them we couldn't put an end to this.

I also decided that if she had a close friend in the class, maybe it would be easier. I thought about the girls at daycare and about talking to their moms to see if they wanted to join the class. Then I thought about this adorable, polite little girl in the class named Karsyn and decided maybe we could try a playdate with her. I would talk to her mom, and maybe I could make a friend out of this too. I felt better. I felt like I was trying.

The next Wednesday came, and P didn't want to go. We really struggled, and I then told her she didn't have to go. For the first time, I gave in to her and told her she could skip. I couldn't bear to make her do this anymore. About five minutes before the class started, she changed her mind, so we ran out of the house and got there just in time. She went into the room willingly. I sat in the waiting room and thought maybe it was over. Maybe it was fine now. I sat there relieved. I told myself this was good. I then decided to sneak around to the other door to see how it was going. It appeared to be ok, but while I was over there, I could hear that same little girl talking to another child about Paisley only having one hand. I thought, Seriously? Girl, give it up. Get over this.

I said nothing and decided to go back to the waiting room. While I was headed there, I ran into the owner, and she asked if I wanted to speak to the girls like we had talked about on the phone. I said sure. I then entered the room and recognized one of my mom's old friends and her daughter watching her granddaughter. I immediately was feeling anxious. It was their first day in the class, and they were going to be listening to me talk about Paisley. I said to myself, "Sure, they're going to think I'm that crazy mother that needs to push her child's handicap on everyone else."

Who knows what they thought of me, and it doesn't matter now. I did what I thought was right and they didn't have the whole story. Also, maybe they didn't think a thing about it. I sat down in a circle with the girls and told them that Paisley was just fine. Yes, she only had one hand, but that was the way God made her, and that was the end of it. None of the girls had a question, and for the most part they just looked at me, so the owner and the instructors thought that was the end of it—that the kids were over it. I, however, was skeptical.

After class that night, I approached Linda, Karsyn's mother, and briefly explained the situation. We exchanged numbers and made a plan. I was so excited. "This is going to be great," I told myself.

Over the next few days, we weren't able to make a playdate work, because of schedules and sickness, etc. We then skipped a week of class. I can't remember why. It ended up that Karsyn was going to attend Paisley's birthday party. Linda and Karsyn came to the party, and it went great. The girls played so great together, and I was so happy. Linda and I also had a few minutes to chat about the situation, and I was so grateful for her willingness to help us. It meant the world to me.

Approaching the next dance class, Paisley was a little hesitant, but she was willing to go. Russell wasn't home from work yet, so Jeten came along too. When we arrived, she entered the classroom with the other girls, and the door closed. About twenty minutes later, the door opened, and Paisley came out with an instructor. She was crying and wanting her mama. Jeten and I talked to her, and she calmed down and agreed to go back in.

As she was going back in with the instructor, Jet said, "Mom, she doesn't want to be in there because of that *one* girl."

I did my best to hush him, embarrassed because the other mother wasn't sitting that far from us and probably heard him. The waiting room was maybe 150 square feet.

I whispered in his ear, "Honey, we don't talk about other people. Her mom is sitting in this room too, and it's rude for us to talk about her baby. We probably hurt her feelings."

Not fifteen minutes later, the whole episode happened again. Paisley came out crying. I agreed to take her home.

Jeten announced, "It's *that* girl's fault."

I was positive the mother heard him this time. I was so embarrassed that I immediately scooped everything up, and we ran out the door, putting coats on along the way. I'm sure the little girl's mother knew nothing at all about the situation. She hadn't witnessed any of the things I had. I have no idea if she witnessed anything at all. I can only assume that the little girl went home talking about Paisley, because she'd appeared so fascinated for the last seven or eight weeks. I had no clue what the other mother knew, but I was pretty sure she now knew that my daughter hated dance class because of hers. I felt horrible for everyone involved.

Needless to say, we didn't return to dance class, and if you speak of dance class to Paisley now, she refuses to talk to you. She still loves to dance and performs all over our home, her safe place.

My niece Annabel joined that dance company in 2015, and Monica was talking to one of the instructors there (not one that ever had Paisley). The instructor mentioned that Monica's niece, meaning Paisley, had attended there before but it hadn't worked out. Apparently Monica said, "Well, I don't think it's quite that simple."

I'm not sure of the rest of the conversation, but Monica at some point was able to make it known that it didn't work out because of Paisley's hand.

The instructor said, "Oh, that's so sad. I just feel so bad for them."

I don't want anyone to take anything away from this experience except awareness. Yes it is sad, but be aware of what's going on around you or with your own children, and caution them that everyone is different, and teach them not to push them about their differences.

I still long for the little girl in dance class, in the adorable tutus and costumes, performing on stage, but I understand that at this time that's not possible. Hopefully Paisley will outgrow this and find her peace with dance class and find the activity that she belongs in. I keep hoping that I can get her to understand that experience wasn't dance class, that it doesn't have to be those girls, that instructor, that studio, etc., that it can be positive. They have restructured the class and the class now doesn't have such a wide age range of children, which is huge. At that time, Paisley was three, and those girls had to be in kindergarten, which just wasn't a good mix no matter the circumstances.

Always pray to have eyes that see the best in people, a heart that forgives the worst, a mind that forgets the bad, and a soul that never loses faith in God.-

—Anonymous

CHAPTER 10

Summers

Playgrounds, pools, and strangers.

We have had so many incidents with children, adolescents, and even adults. It seriously amazes me what people will say to us and to her. The number of people that talk about her to their friends or parents in front of her astounds me as well. She's not hard of hearing, and she hears everything you say about her and understands it. This also applies to people that are old enough to know better.

I remember two adolescent boys at a pool playground when Paisley wasn't very old but old enough to hear them and know they were talking about her. They were playing catch and one of them missed the ball and it ended up by us, so they came close enough to see her, and one said to the other, "Dude, look at her. She only has one hand."

The other one said, "Yeah, that's crazy. So sad." And off they went.

They had their little chat within about fifteen feet of us. Sometimes it's appropriate for me to speak up, and sometimes it's just better to ignore it.

One Spring afternoon, I was having coffee with a friend at a local coffee shop that happens to be inside a church with an indoor playground, perfect for mothers to have coffee and kids to play. The friend and I were chatting, and I realized that a little boy was trying to approach Paisley. Immediately, my mother bear kicked in, and I watched very intently as he was desperately trying to catch her to touch her. I walked into the playground and suggested she go to the bathroom. She agreed she needed to go. As we were walking there, I told her that she didn't need to talk to anyone she didn't want to and no one was ever allowed to touch her without her permission.

I said, "P, you can tell them anything you like. You can tell them to mind their business. You can tell them they're rude. Or you can simply walk away. But you don't need to talk to them if you don't want." I also told her in the course of the conversation that I would be watching and to come get me if she needed me. That little boy maybe wasn't old enough to know better, but his mother was in the room too, not saying anything to him, so I was hoping that Paisley, armed with her words, could teach him to back off. I don't know exactly what she said to him, but I was watching as he approached again a little later, and then he backed off a bit, but soon thereafter she was ready to leave. Sometimes that is just easiest for us— to walk away. Trying to educate is exhausting; even though it's important, we can only take so much.

One summer on our annual camping trip to South Dakota, we took a ride on an antique fire truck that the campground owns. It was just us four that afternoon. We boarded the truck and were waiting for everyone else to get seated. An older gentleman and his granddaughter sat across from us. As we were riding around seeing the sights at the campground, the man said to me, "What happened to her?"

That question always puzzles me, especially from adults, because if you're starring at her enough to know she's missing her hand, you should be able to see that it's not a clean cut—that there is a little fist there with teeny fingers, and therefore, nothing "happened" to her. I gave him my normal response: "That's just the way God made her." Once again, as I usually do, I thought, What if something *had* happened to her? What if her arm had been amputated? Do you really think it would be something we'd want to talk about to a perfect stranger? It would more than likely be either a freak accident or a disease, neither of which makes for pleasant small talk.

During that same camping trip in South Dakota, we had an abundance of incidents. For the most part, it's the same trip every year, same sights and places, so I don't know if we're noticing it more now that she's older or what, but it was bad this year. On our last day at the campground, everyone in our group was napping except Paisley and me, so we headed to the pool for the third time that day. As we were walking down the steps to enter the pool, a little boy said something to her (I can't quite recall what it was), and she didn't even respond to him. She just gazed up at me with a sad, sad face and said, "Mama, why do they ask that too much?" She'd had it with people, and I couldn't blame her.

I scooped her up and held her close, as both our hearts were breaking.

As we swam, I said, "Honey, I'm so, so sorry. I really don't know why people always ask you that. I'm sorry, baby. I love you so much, and I am so very proud of you."

Shortly thereafter, there was lightning and we had to evacuate the pool. As we were gathering our things to leave the area, a lifeguard approached us. I recognized him from being there the last few days. He said, "Your daughter has the most amazing spirit. I was watching her yesterday on the waterslide and was inspired by her. She's wonderful."

I said, "Thank you so much. That was so nice of you. She's definitely full of spirit."

That right there is what I wish people would see about her, what I want people to say to us. It really meant a lot to hear that. This chapter may sound a little contradictory because I'm pushing for education and yet complaining about all the questions, but it's probably a perfect example of how hard it can be on her. The questions are so hard on her. She desperately wants to be normal and accepted. A great example of why acceptance is so important: If it was more widely accepted, people wouldn't need to ask all the questions. They could see past her differences and see her remarkable spirit.

Since being graced with Paisley, my needs have changed. I now need to be an advocate for my child. Instead of wanting to change Paisley to fit into the world, I want to change the world for Paisley. I have found my place in the world and, together with her brothers, she has taught me to be the mother that I am today.

CHAPTER 11

Safe Spaces

I've mentioned before that having a safe space for Paisley to go at all times where she feels comfortable to be her, to be who she is, who God made her, is so incredibly important. Our home is number one and we do our best to always make sure that it feels safe for her, and it is the place to go when she needs a break from the world.

She has always had a room that was hers, whether it was upstairs in the beginning or now downstairs it is so important to her. That is her number one safe space, and we allow her to take all the time she needs to process in there no matter what the circumstances. There have been multiple times in her life where there has been an incident involving other people or something that made her feel so uncomfortable that she instantly demanded to go home. Straight home with no stops. One time we even had another child with us and Paisley had to get dropped off at our house before the other child could get dropped off at theirs because she so desperately needed her safe space.

We have always tried our very best to make sure our camper also has that same feeling for Paisley, and during the summers, we drag it around the country and have wonderful adventures, but when P has had too much of the outside world, she enters her playroom in the camper for a movie, or she plays there for hours, either by herself or with a girlfriend. I'm so glad that she feels safe, secure, and happy somewhere, because the world can be so cruel. We have encountered many mean, difficult comments on our adventures, and I love that she is strong enough to remove herself and be safe in her space.

I don't enjoy camping with strangers for this very reason as it can be hard on Paisley, and I try to look at our camping trips as breaks for her. We enjoy camping with our family and close friends. I know it sounds terrible, but it's so very important that she gets breaks and has a safe place.

She has been dealing with people and their comments her whole life already, just about everywhere we go. She continues to deal with it even today and if there is the slightest amount of control that I can have to ensure my child is happy and safe I will do it even if it means not including others in our adventures. She is "different," and that is not changing and until we can change people's perceptions and commentary, and acceptance levels, safe spaces are where we want to be any chance we get.

I know that my controlling nature is hard to comprehend, because I should look at these situations as awareness—awareness by making people aware that they are judging her, that it can be hurtful, and often bystanders will be aware as well—but I really don't want them when we are trying to spend time together as a family, we get enough of it every other day.

I will always do everything in my power to make sure my child has a safe space. The schools have been very accommodating with this as well and they often have a safe corner or space in every classroom Paisley is ever in.

All around the world, home, school, or camping adventures, safe spaces are so incredibly important for mental well-being.

Often we pray to God in times of trouble, when we are at our worst, but we need to remember that we should pray to him with thanks on our good days as well.

CHAPTER 12

Questions from the Heart

I remember that before Paisley turned one, she knew she was different. As a baby, maybe eight months old, she would sit on the floor and examine her arms, looking at the differences. I remember her looking at everyone and looking at herself and knowing the difference. It was not something we taught her; it was something she knew from early on. Once she started speaking, she started asking questions. The older she got, the more frequent and in depth the questions became.

I remember an incident at daycare that was retold to me by the provider. Donna and Paisley had been playing catch with stuffed toy snowballs. Paisley announced that she wished she could throw and catch like Donna. She wished she had two hands. This is something that we hear often to this day, but Donna hadn't heard it before. It's hard on everyone around her, and you just have to take it in stride and explain to her that it was God's plan and that she does amazing with the arms she has and that she is meant for greatness.

One Friday in July 2015 I picked the kids up early in the afternoon. We were headed out to go camping for the weekend. Russell was hooking everything up so that when I arrived with the kids we could hop in the pickup and take off. As we were driving the short distance home, Paisley said, "Mama, when I going to get my other hand?"

We didn't have plans to attend Shriners again yet, so I said, "What hand, baby?"

"Well, when I getting two hands like you and everyone has."

I was suddenly ill. "Baby, I am so sorry, but you have the hands that God gave you."

Her mood changed; she was *mad*. "I don't want this hand. I want ones like everyone." She went on with her fit about no one else being like her and not wanting her hand.

Jeten piped up from the seat next to her. "Mom, there's other girls like Sissy. Right, Mom?" Thank God for Jeten Wyman.

"Yes, that's right, honey. There are other kids like you, Sis."

Paisley said, "Well where are them's houses?"

I immediately thought about some of the social media accounts that I have found to be a huge support and resource to me and I said, "Baby, I'm not exactly sure, but I promise you I will find someone you can meet that is just like you."

The best kind of people are the ones that come into your life and make you see the sun where you once saw clouds. The people that believe in you so much that you start to believe in you too. The people that love you, simply for being you. The once in a lifetime kind of people.

—Anonymous

CHAPTER 13

Shriners: Take 2

In 2015 we decided to take Paisley back to Shriners. It had been close to three years since we'd been there, and Paisley had been feeling very self-conscious, so I felt that if we were able to show her some options, she might have a better understanding of what she might need, and maybe if we got her a passive hand to wear in public, she might feel less uncomfortable. We still didn't really see her struggling with anything but truly felt it was our duty as her parents to stay educated and try everything we could for her. We decided to take the Abells (Russell's sister Monica, her husband, Greg, and their kids, Annabel and Emmit) along and make a trip out of it, staying at the cabin (my parents' home in Park Rapids, MN) and day tripping to Minneapolis. And I really wanted to bring Jet to Minnesota for the cabin weekend but wanted to just take Paisley to the appointment so we could really focus on her and her needs.

The Abells agreed to come to Minnesota, and they'd come along to Minneapolis and just keep Jet at the mall while we went to the appointment. And then we could meet back up at the zoo later, if the appointment didn't take too long. Paisley loves aquariums, so we got on the road early Thursday morning to hit up the aquarium before her appointment. We arrived with just barely enough time to get through the aquarium, eat a snack, and head for the appointment. There was a lot happening at the mall that day, and I felt bad that Paisley had to leave to go to the doctor.

We arrived at the appointment and spent most of our time in orthopedics, learning about the different options. We were very fortunate that there was another family there with a child just like Paisley, and there had been a complication with his arm fitting that day, otherwise they wouldn't have still been there, but God works in mysterious ways, and they agreed to chat with us while they were waiting. They were in the playground area, so we went out and the orthotics lady, Megan, introduced us and we learned all about Andre and his story.

We learned they had found out prior to his birth and had him on a prosthetic path at one month of age. It was so amazing to connect with this family and ask questions. They were extremely knowledgeable and a huge asset to us. It was amazing that just a small little hiccup in the day for them could result in such a major event to us.

After our meeting with them and watching Andre's fittings take place, Paisley agreed to be cast for an arm of her own. It was a big achievement for her, and we were so proud that even though she was so tired she was willing to be cast. They took several measurements and then put a cast on her arm, then we picked her skin tone and took the reading materials. It's so crazy to pick out a limb for your child, something you don't really think about having to do in your life.

After the appointment we met back up with the Abells at the Como Zoo, which is a wonderful place. I found by then that I had almost checked out for the day. I walked along and looked at the animals but was extremely reserved. It had been such an emotional day and experience. Paisley seemed to be feeling about the same. After the zoo, we headed for supper and back to the cabin.

The next morning I arose early. Park Rapids area is such a beautiful place, and I love a good morning walk to start the day. Russell and the kids were still sleeping, so I could sneak out of the house. All of the Abells were awake, but Monica could escape, since Greg was willing to stay with their kids.

Monica joined me, and it ended up being great inspiration. I spoke to her about the appointment the day before, how great it was to meet the other family, and how amazing God was in that tiny little moment. I spoke to her about my feelings and fears. She didn't say too much, mostly just listened to me, which was great, but she did assure me that she thought we were making the right choice to move forward with the arm, and she agreed that all we could do was try. We had an enjoyable rest of the weekend at the cabin, with little to no talk of the arm.

When we returned home, though, I started talking to her about it and how she was feeling and if she wanted an arm like Andre had. I also showed her pictures of Lauren Scruggs Kennedy a model/blogger that had been in a terrible accident in December 2011 and who now wears a prosthetic passive arm in public. I explained to Paisley that Lauren had an arm like her, but she wears her other arm in public so that people don't ask her as many questions. I thought that might speak to her, but I was unsure. At this point, though, I felt it was important to proceed, since we had the casting, and construction had begun. Plus I wanted her to see it.

We did a lot of talking in the next couple months with Paisley and our family and friends. Over our September camping trip to Medora, I had an opportunity to chat with my friend Melini. It was a similar conversation to the one I had with Monica, but it was so great to have the support of our family and friends. It's so helpful in times like these to reach out to our support system. I truly felt like we were making the right path by at least trying something.

Paisley's arm was ready in late September, but we chose to go back over during the teacher's convention on October 23, since the kids would be out of school and I would have to be off from work. I felt it was important for Paisley to have her brother for support that day, so Jeten came to Minneapolis and the appointments with us.

The first thing Paisley said when they put the arm on her for the first time was, "Mom, when will I get the one where the fingers move?"

Instantly heartbroken, I explained to her that she had to commit to wearing this one for a whole year and wearing it regularly before she could upgrade to the moving (myoelectric) fingers. It was hard for her to understand a whole year, but we were doing our best with her. The fitting went really well, though, and we chose one attachment for the new arm, as the passive hand would unscrew for more tools, depending on needs.

We chose what we refer to as the "Lego hand," since that's what it reminds us of. We thought it would be good for fishing, since it would help her hold her pole. She was able to spend limited time with the OT department, which I was disappointed about, but they were busy that day and there was a lot of waiting time and the kids were restless.

After the appointment, we ran a couple errands and hit the road back to the Park Rapids cabin, our haven in the woods. My parents were there that weekend, which was nice, and we had a great weekend. Paisley didn't wear the arm much, but once we were home with it, we tried to reward her for wearing it. It wasn't something she was used to, so in some ways it was a burden to her. I tried to bribe her to wear it, which I was told by Kelli (Andre's mom) is perfectly fine, and the OT agreed that you do whatever you have to. We were taking it at her pace, and for the most part she was wearing it once a day for a few minutes. It's less now, which I'm sad about, but we're committed to being there for her and not pushing her. I had been making a huge effort to leave it under foot where I knew she would find it, and I occasionally would find her wearing it. She really only wore the "Lego" end, for a long time which was fine with me. It's hers to do with as she chooses. I had been purposely putting it in her underwear drawer for a while, as I know that she opens it daily, but she wasn't impressed, now I just try to leave it in her path. Recently she switched to the passive hand end and now has only had that ending on. I still feel that even though she doesn't need it, and doesn't wear it regularly, we made the right choice to try something, and it will be up to her how we proceed.

"May the strength of God pilot us. May the wisdom of God instruct us. May the hand of God protect us. May the word of God direct us."

—Saint Patrick

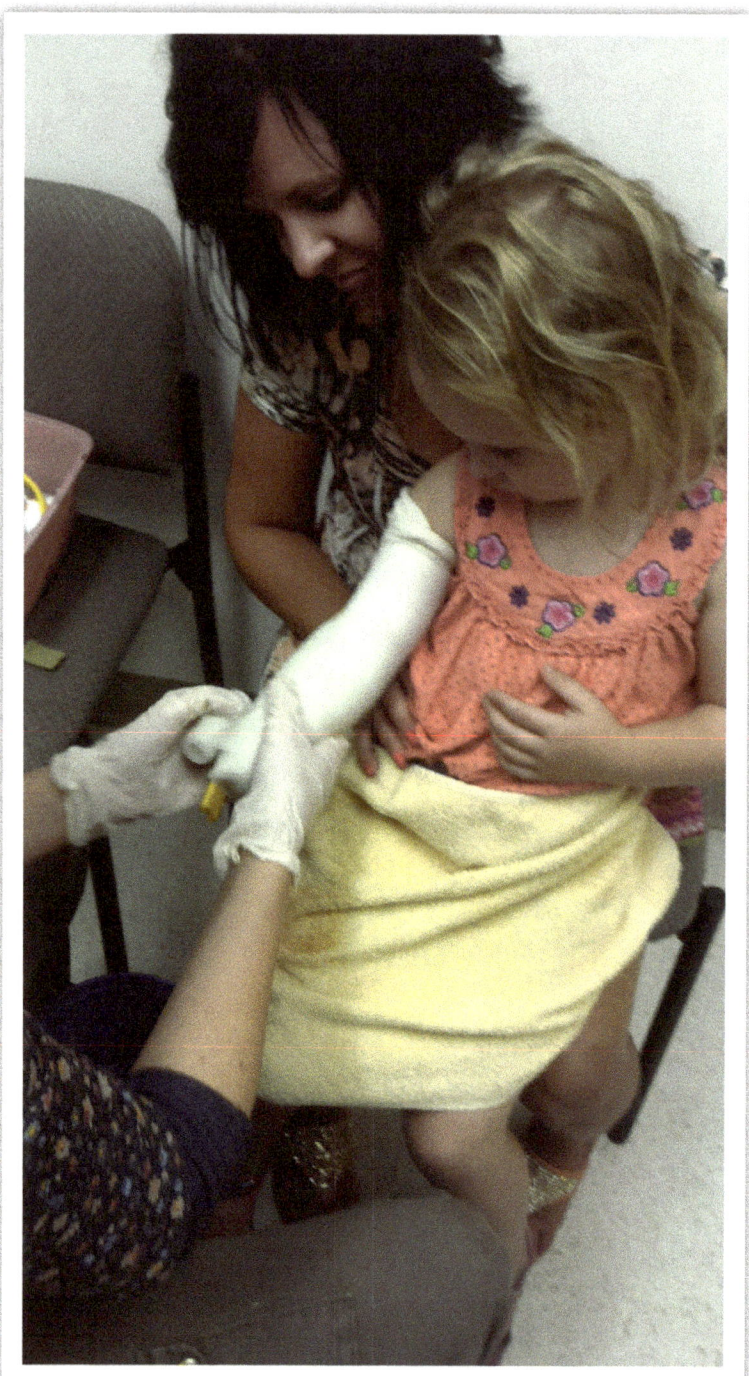

CHAPTER 14

New Environments

Since finding full-time daycare for both kids at the same place in June of 2012, when Paisley was about seven months old and Jeten about nineteen months, we hadn't made any changes. August 2015, they began some acting out with the daycare lady in her home, and I truly felt it was time to find some more structure for them, especially for Paisley. When she's bored or lacking stimulation, she tends to look for mischief. She'd managed to get hold of a can of paint and dump it on the poor woman's carpet. Needless to say, that was the episode that really spoke to me.

I began looking for places to send them and came upon a full-time preschool that had some openings. We already had a part-time preschool scheduled for this year but thought we could switch and try a full-time center. I had my reservations, though. Everyone at the current daycare had known Paisley since she was a baby, and here I was pulling her out of the safe comfort and sending her into the world. I was so nervous, and I thought so very hard about the decision, but in the end we moved forward, and we started in September, after Labor Day.

The first few days were rough. Both kids came home every day talking about all the kids that had asked about Paisley's arm. They didn't seem to be enjoying it at all. It was a change of environment, structure, and familiarity. I felt terrible about it but thought if we could get past the first few days, the newness of her would wear off for the other kids. One day when I picked them up, I asked Jet how the day was.

"Awful," he said.

"How come, honey? Don't you like it there?"

"No, all the kids are naughty."

"Naughty? What do they do?"

"They ask about Sissy's arm all day," he said.

"Oh, they aren't naughty. They're just curious about her. They've never seen her before. It will get better. I promise."

We held on, and eventually they seemed to fit in and complained less about the arm questions. New places are always so hard. I know she'll have those feelings forever, but I think the experiences she gained that year have been huge in terms of socializing her and building strength.

I have a bracelet from Lenny & Eva and it helps me to remember how important it is to be strong in life:

Here's to strong women
May we know them
May we be them
May we raise them

CHAPTER 15

Activities

Fall 2015, Jeten went back to hockey, and he and Paisley started private swim lessons, since the only classes for their age are held during the day and I work. I tried getting her into dance again, but *dance* was like a swear word at our house, so I didn't push her to do anything. After Christmas, though, I decided she needed to do something—something that could be hers, and we could try a few things until she found hers. I signed her up for tennis. I don't know anything about tennis but I thought we could figure it out. There was a four-week program, and it was so good for her to be in an activity. She was so shy in public and so self-conscious, and we needed to fight that.

She struggled with comparing herself to the other girls, but as far as tennis, if that strong-willed girl of mine was trying, she was great at it! However, anyone who knows Paisley knows that everything is on her terms, and it's her way or the highway. I was proud of her effort nonetheless, and it was so fun spending time together, one on one.

One morning after tennis, we decided to stay at the ARC (Williston Area Recreation Center), and I let her play on the playground a bit. They have an indoor one, and the boys were out ice fishing, so before we headed home, I told her she could play for a minute. When we first arrived, there were only a couple of other children, and it was so nice, but then, all of a sudden, a man arrived with several children, maybe six boys and a girl. I wasn't sure how many were with him and how many just arrived then, but one of them spotted Paisley almost right away. She was at the top of a slide about to go down, and he came up behind her. He was planning to go next.

Immediately he exclaimed to his friend or brother, "Look at her arm!"

Paisley slid down the slide, and the boy was just in shock. He didn't go down the slide. He saw her run across to the other side of the playground, so he headed there over the bridge, just flabbergasted by her. He was screaming, "Look! Look! That is awful!"

That's when I got up from my spot and walked across the playground to this scene. I looked up at him as he was starring P down, and before he could say anything more, I told him he was being pretty rude and that was enough.

He proceeded to argue with me. "But it's awful."

I said, "No, it isn't. It's the way God made her, and she's just fine."

"But it's sooo weird."

Again I said, "No, it is not, and that's enough from you."

I asked Paisley if she was ready to leave yet, and she wasn't, but as she went to play on a climbing rock, she realized other kids were looking at her, and she was ready to leave.

We proceeded to the car, and I was hot. It was definitely a mama bear moment. Once in the car and buckled up, P asked if we could have "Shake It Off," meaning she wanted to hear the Taylor Swift song, "Shake It Off" on the radio.

Tears welled in my eyes at the thought of the maturity in this four-year-old, as well as her courage and strength.

As we got ready to drive away, I was itching to do something, say something, but I couldn't quite get my thoughts together. I didn't want the crazy mom post on Facebook. Then it hit me—education moment. I found a picture of one of Paisley's favorite books, *It's Okay to Be Different*, and I posted that to Facebook with this caption: "Educate your kids! It's ok to be different!! We LOVE this book at our house. Just explained to a little one on the playground that my daughter's arm isn't awful or weird and she's fine the way God made her. ♡"

I read this on a wall somewhere, wrote it down, and it has stuck with me:

Mothers
Believe in us more than we believe in ourselves
Do more for us than they do for themselves
Worry about us more than we realize
Pray for us more than we'll ever know
Value us more than anything else in the world
Give us more than they can afford
Love us more than anyone else can
Matter more than words can express

CHAPTER 16

From the Mom

To say that I have a different outlook on life is an understatement. Having kids in general forces you to see the world differently, but I feel that I've seen things even more differently since Paisley's birth. I look at the world differently than I used to and in no way could have imagined.

Recently we had an adult weekend out of town with another couple. It was so nice to get away, even just for one night. We attended a hockey game in Grand Forks, something we try to do once a year, and Russell knows the right people to get excellent tickets. This year, shortly after we arrived at the arena, we were in line to get wristbands so we could drink alcohol.

As my turn was approaching, one of the women working there announced to those in line, "Have your ID ready, and the wristband goes on your right hand."

I walked away thinking, What if you don't have a right hand? It was such a simple statement—just as simple as ten fingers and ten toes—but it left me pondering. I find that I think those things often, and I probably will forever. I know that people don't mean any harm in those statements, but it leaves me wanting more from this world.

I desperately want acceptance for my daughter. I want to walk through the grocery store or an airport and not think about her anxiety or watch the people stare. I want it to be completely normal for all children to be different in some way. Ever since my kids started preschool I have always enjoyed seeing what they're learning, and I love all of their creations, as I'm sure every mother does. I love picking them up and seeing the excitement from them in what they've created.

A few years ago, a valentine came home from each of my babies. It was so sweet. They were heart-shaped cutouts with their traced left and right hands in the middle and a sweet sentiment. I saw Jeten's first and thought it was adorable. I didn't think a thing about his two hands being traced. I came across P's later and was slightly disappointed. Hers was also a heart-shaped paper with two hands traced inside. I wasn't sure how they had done it, maybe she used the same hand and just flipped it over, or maybe it was another child's hand? I made a comment to my husband about it, and his response was that they probably wanted hers to look the same as everyone else's. That may be the case. I wasn't there that day, and I don't know what she said or what they said. Maybe it was even her idea to have two hands on the valentine. I wanted both of *her* hands, though. I didn't really say much to her about it. You never know what her response will be anyway. She often says the opposite of the truth in these situations.

I find that sometimes when I try to have heart-to-heart conversations about a situation that happened or something that I'm feeling with a confidant, the chosen friend really doesn't grasp what I'm saying. I don't complain about P's situations very often, but sometimes I'm having a bad day, and I want to vent, and sometimes people want to blow it off, or I can tell they are not listening, like I'm overreacting and it isn't that big a deal—that it's not that big a deal that my daughter only has one hand. It could be much worse. Yes, very true. It could be, and we know that, and we don't want to change a thing about her, but that doesn't mean there aren't struggles and heartaches.

I haven't found very many people that I can talk to. I'm so grateful to have met Kelli and that I have had her to lean on over the years and I follow other mothers on social media. It's so important to not feel alone and to know that there are other people out there just like you. I'm blessed with an understanding family, and I am grateful for that too. They do their best to understand what it's like, and I would guess that, for the most part, everyone in our family or anyone close to us has had a P situation of their own.

My mom recently told me that she was thinking about things to teach the kids—things she had taught to my brother and me. And she was thinking they were probably old enough for this nursery rhyme and hand movements: "Here is the church. Here is the steeple. Open the doors, and see all the people."

As she thought deeper about it, she chose not to bring it up to them, since Paisley wouldn't be able to do it. I feel for people in those situations. I know what those feelings are like, and it hurts the heart.

A couple years ago someone told me that she had witnessed Paisley at daycare and saw that her long sleeve was bothering her. So Paisley had asked one of the teachers to help her roll it up. She said the exchange was heartwarming. The teacher was more than willing to help her and appeared to think nothing about it. The person telling me the story thought it was a wonderful moment to witness and wanted me to know how sweet it was. All of our lives aren't about complaining or about the can'ts. More often than not they are about compassion and understanding for other people, forcing ourselves to think about others, and wanting to make sure people know it's ok to be different. Kindness costs nothing.

"Life is too short to wake up in the morning with regrets. Love the people who treat you right, forgive the ones who don't, and believe everything happens for a reason."

—Anonymous

CHAPTER 17

Dance take 2

January 2016 with the help of the Abell ladies we were able to convince Paisley to go back to dance class and that is all I really wanted. If she went back and then decided she didn't want to dance that would have been fine with me I just wanted her to know that the other class and other people were not "dance class." There are other classes and other girls. We went back to the same studio that we had been at before and the same one that Annabel had joined the previous Fall. This time dance class was a success! The class had been restructured and the kids were all about the same age. Paisley may have been one of the older ones by a couple months which may have helped this time around as well. It was also huge to have her cousin and bestie Annabel in the class as well as some other girls she knew and she quickly made new friends. She enjoyed going, seeing her friends and picking out her dance outfit each week. She did whine about going sometimes but this time it was about being a tired little old girl and not about her arm. She finished out the dance year in May and I was so very proud of her. She attended one of the summer princess classes and joined again Fall of 2016. She had her first dance recital November 11th 2016 and she did amazing. She got up on that stage and shined. She grinned from ear to ear and you could tell she was so proud of herself and didn't have a care in the world. She twirled with confidence and I watched with tears in my eyes. This little girl has come so far in life making her own way. She has carried and still does carry so much anxiety and yet in the right setting can be so incredibly confident. I so admire her confidence and her ability to power through her feelings.

She has continued dance and performed in more recitals. This past Fall she was in Jazz but recently switched to a Tap class.

"She is clothed in strength and dignity"

—Proverbs 31:25

CHAPTER 18

Expansion

2015 started with me being consumed by wanting to expand the family, for many reasons I did not think I wanted to be pregnant again. Ever since I was a teen I've wanted to adopt a child and kicked off 2015 with research. I can be like a dog with a bone when I get an idea or am hunting for something. I narrowed it down to a Christian agency in Indiana and made contact with them. They have a school age exchange program that I looked into first and ultimately decided I wanted to adopt from a Philippine orphanage. They are almost backwards from every other country out there in that they want an almost perfect match between child and family and actually match you first before moving forward into getting approved to adopt. We did start with the initial background and investigation but did not have to have a home study done before we picked the child. They started sending us tons of information and lists. It was gut-wrenching essentially "shopping" for a child. By mid-April we were matched with an adorable little boy and moving forward. However it didn't take long and he was wanted by someone in his home country and then it was game over, doesn't matter where you are in the process they get first choice. I was devastated, from the instant that we were told we had pled our case well and were matched I believed he was ours and put my heart into him. However I was still on the path of expansion and pulled out the latest list of babes. We then came across information about an adorable 2 year old girl she was younger than we were thinking about but she jumped out at us from the pages of information. She was born limb different just like Paisley and it seemed meant to be. Of all the kids in the world this one was on the page looking just like our little girl, she was wearing Minnie mouse sunglasses and looking sassy as can be just like P. She was born without a left hand instead of Paisley born without the right. As we dug into her story a bit more we learned she had been found in a garbage can. A garbage can!! There was absolutely nothing wrong with her she was simply thrown away because she was born without two hands. Wow did that make us feel every feeling you can imagine... Sad, Anger, Heartache, Sick... the list goes on. It was so hard to imagine someone bearing this child and simply throwing her away. I looked at our amazing Paisley and thought wow they didn't know what they were missing. We were never matched with this little girl as she was spoken for before it was our turn to pick again. I hope whoever has her that they are a real family and she is flourishing, sharing her gifts with the world. I imagine her being just like Paisley except with dark hair and brown eyes.

Next we decided to take a break and explore other options it was Russell's turn to choose our path and he was convinced that there were children in our own backyard that could use us too so we started looking into it. I was adamant that we stick with children without legal guardians, wards of states. We met with North Dakota September 15th 2015 and were immediately sent to 27 hours of parenting classes before moving forward. Oddly enough there was a class starting in our hometown within a few weeks that qualified. We then secretly began spending our Saturdays at PRIDE training. We had told our families almost nothing that we had been up to for months and until something concrete transpired we felt it was best. PRIDE is mostly directed at fostering children, children in foster care or living in a guardianship with grandparents, relatives or friends. We took the class with several other couples almost all of them foster parents that had foster children placed in their homes. I had been adamant that I was not fostering I checked the "No" box several times on several occassions. On the last day of PRIDE there was a panel of foster parents that you could ask anything you wanted. Russell fired off questions right and left and at one point I turned to him and said "we're becoming foster parents aren't we?"

After PRIDE was over I called ND and told them our classes were done and asked what was next. Next she said that they would need to do a home study and they were pretty backed up it was going to be May before they had time. May! That was 6 months from now and to me I had already been at it all of 2015, I know I had just barely started with them but I felt defeated. I then began brainstorming that if I became a foster parent I could potentially get placed with a child without legal guardians and could start the adoption process that way as a lot of children without legal guardians are in foster care. At the very least I could potentially have the child living with us even if he wasn't a Wyman yet.

December 2015 bring on the foster paperwork. Our license was official February 2016 and within days we were getting calls. Several calls before a placement worked out. First we took in a baby even though we didn't think we wanted a baby but little did we know God had his own plan (we should be used to that by now). It's funny how God turns your plans upside down and backwards and gets you to want something you didn't know you wanted. For some reason he was able to convince me that I wanted another Wyman baby I was terrified and anxious but entertaining the idea and before I knew it I was pregnant. Pregnant with Wyman baby number three was definitely different than one and two. For one I was older. For two I had several children by then, J & P, foster baby and seven year old foster girl. Mostly baby number three just brought more anxiety. I was so concerned about how he was doing and what he was going to look like. I was consumed by thoughts of "how many fingers?" and "how many toes?" I had several ultrasounds with him and each and every one I asked if they could see any of his fingers. We were never able to count to 10 so until he was born I was not sure. We even had an ultrasound late one night in the emergency room just a few days before he was born and we couldn't see. I felt so guilty that night it was late and the technician had worked all day but was also on call and they had apparently had several patients, I could tell he was exhausted and wanted to go home but he was so patient and caring with us and obliged our want to try to count fingers after he collected the data he was after. We were so appreciative to him for being understanding and supportive. In the end though does it really matter? Yes, Maverick Russell Evans was born January 5th 2017 with 10 fingers and 10 toes and we are grateful but Paisley has shown us that it really doesn't matter, she is a master of life and You Don't Need 10.

God grant me the serenity to accept the things I cannot change, the courage to change the things I can and the wisdom to know the difference.

—Serenity Prayer

CHAPTER 19

Life Skills

I've said it before but our way of seeing the world has also changed. We were in Park Rapids at the cabin one Spring, and I was in the middle of making a map for work, the family was all around and my parents had just made a meal I can't recall exactly maybe patty melts? Regardless it was a sandwich of some kind and if I recall a messy one. Russ was holding the baby and he was sleeping peacefully. He tried to get me to hold him and I said I really need to get this project done he frowned a little but understood. I then realized that he was going to eat one of the sandwiches so I said I could hold the baby and work at the same time. Russ said he was fine he could do both. I then said "don't you need two hands to eat that?" "No, I don't need two hands for anything." Well said Russ, well said. His comment stopped me dead in my tracts. I felt guilty for it and often do in situations like that. I always immediately think of P, often when talking to a kid and they have something they need to hold steady I'll say "use both hands" I've said it to P a hundred times without thinking.

However, she does actually do it and since she has a wrist and a fist it's appropriate but it's those take for granted phrases that catch me sometimes.

Paisley has always wanted to tackle the world the same way everyone does and more often than not you can't help her with a thing. Sometimes she will ask for help when she doesn't need it but it's for attention and we all know it. If it's something that she is trying to learn you cannot help her. Her preschool teachers said the same thing. They would watch her sometimes trying to do a project and want to help her and she would refuse. Once they got to know her better they wouldn't even ask her they'd just watch. I remember them telling me one time that there are days they want to help her and know she doesn't want the help just as there are kids nagging them for help that have two hands and really shouldn't need the help. She has managed to master every skill she has tackled. If it's a marker lid (or lipstick lid ☺) she will use the crook of her arm to hold the cap end and then pull hard to get the lid off. She can handle opening anything, scissors, rulers, anything arts and crafts related she is always creating something. Paisley is a very busy determined girl! Recently she talked me into press on nails at the grocery and I obliged. She manages to put them on herself. Shocked me to say the least, I did them the first time but they never last and she always has them on and off. First time I watched I was amazed as I usually am by her... She lines them up on the counter lines her finger up tucks it under the end of the fake nail then guides it the rest of the way with her right fist and uses that fist to press it on her left fingers and away she goes.

Last year we were pushing her to figure out coats, hats, gloves, etc as we knew this year in kindergarten she was going to need to know how to do it. The teacher's aide does not need to be helping her get dressed every day twice a day (or more) for recess. A huge accomplishment but she managed to figure out zippers. A proud, proud moment! I remember her telling people too that she could now zip up her own coat and there wasn't too much reaction which I found interesting; think about it... this kid with 1 hand just managed to zip up her coat! As the mom I felt it should have made the evening news. She worked for a long, long time on zippers and I still remember the day she first did it! To do it she steadily rests the right side of the coat on her leg and holds it down with her right fist and then uses her left had to work the zipper into place and then steadily starts to zip it still holding it down a bit with the right fist. She is so impressive she can teach herself anything and she has since she was a baby. I remember her barely a year and a half old sitting in the high chair and eating peaches, all of a sudden she started using her left hand to rest the peach on her right arm and then steadily guided it to her mouth and was feeding herself with the right arm. Without causing too much raucous I was able to get the camera and video tape it. Such a shaping moment and a foretaste of the life she leads now.

CHAPTER 20

Kindergarten

Summer of 2017, once Paisley realized it was real, she had graduated preschool and was heading to the "big school" she became anxious. Several times over the summer she had **major** meltdowns about how life was hard for her and she would literally say "Why is life so hard for me?", "Why do I have to go to a new school again?" and "Why do I have to meet new friends?" The week we spent at the Minnesota cabin in July she was very vocal about it and it was heart wrenching she was dreading having to go to Kindergarten and deal with all that was to come, the comments and questions and all the feelings. I came close to calling a therapist I had worked with foster children in the past.

Jeten had Mrs. Rehak for kindergarten at Rickard Elementary and she was amazing the more I have gotten to know her the more I realize how amazing she is all over the earth, we have even become friends, so for Paisley I wanted the same. I don't even know the other teacher at the school so I have no comparison to make but I knew I wanted my friend (Tarren) introducing Paisley to this whole new world.

Shortly before school started in August Tarren suggested we meet for coffee to talk about P, she had been thinking about how to approach the year, a new experience for all of us. She suggested that she take a picture of Paisley to Kindergarten Screening where she could introduce Paisley to every student that was going to be in class with her. Tarren had thought if she showed each child a picture of P and explained that she only has one hand and let them ask questions that it would alleviate some of the initial shock or chaos combined with the start of school. With many emotions I agreed, I thought it was a great idea and was so impressed that she had been putting so much thought into Paisley feeling comfortable in her class. After Kindergarten Screening she reported that it went well and that many of the children already knew Paisley which also made me feel a hundred times better.

Since Kindergarten has started I have heard very little about other people reacting to Paisley's arm and the incidents that have happened Paisley has apparently handled like a champ with grace and courage.

One day during lunch, from what I have pieced together, a couple girls from the other kindergarten class were talking about Paisley and she heard them and I'm not sure what happened next but from there it turned into the other kindergarten teacher asking Paisley if she would like to come to her class and talk to the other kids about her arm. Apparently Paisley agreed and after lunch went to the other kindergarten class and spoke to them about her arm, after it was over her bestie and cousin, Annabel walked her back to her own class.

KINDERGARTEN

Tarren is who first told me about the episode she called me after school and I was shocked to say the very least I could not imagine having the courage at 5 to do something like that. That afternoon when I picked Paisley up she didn't say much and still hasn't but we had dance that night and I usually sit and chat with Monica during dance, Annabel had come home that afternoon and told Monica about it. So from Tarren, Annabel and the couple words from P, I think I have pieced together what happened. I have been so amazed at her and how open and social she has become. I was so terrified of her going to school and having to deal with these issues but with the strength God has given her she can truly handle anything.

A few weeks in she asked me one night if she could wear her arm to school, I said "of course you can, it's your arm you can wear it anywhere you want." She decided the next day to wear it and I was so nervous for her. I get the impression that it was more of a prop or source of conversation than it was useful but I'm glad she felt comfortable enough to show it to the school world. That evening when I came to pick her up from the after school program it was missing however and I was frantic and emotional and quite upset about it. Not because it was missing or that I was even mad at her, it had been a stressful day and I was like seriously I am searching all over the playground and the school for my daughter's arm? Really? Why this? I remember those same feelings from the day that we picked out the arm to begin with who has to pick out an arm for their child? and match skin tone? and who has to search for their kid's arm? Another one of those alone moments. It didn't last long though, not too long after we arrived home I had a message from Halsie the after school director she had continued searching after we left and found it. Paisley has not chosen to wear it to school again it's still an at home tool.

I look forward to what is next for her in school with less worry than before, as her mom I will always worry but in these few short months so far I am as proud as I can be and awed by this beautiful soul.

Family n. (fam-i-ly):

A crazy bunch of people who deeply care for each other. Those who live, laugh, forgive, dance, and love together. People bonded by blood, adoption, marriage or the heart.

Paisley's family

Paisley's mother was born Kathleen Kay Taylor, on March 15, 1984, to Doug and Donnette Taylor, in Williston, North Dakota.

Doug Taylor was born and raised in Mississippi and ventured to North Dakota in 1979 during an oil boom. He met Donnette Polson (born and raised in Williston), and they wed in 1981 in Williston. Doug and Donnette have another child, Perry Taylor who suffers from Traumatic Brain Injury aftereffects of Pediatric Brain Cancer. All currently reside in Williston.

Paisley's mom met her dad, Russell Wyman, in 2000, and they wed in 2006. Russell William Wyman was born May 29, 1981, to Rick and Pam Wyman, in Sidney, Montana. Rick and Pam (Denowh), both originally from Sidney, Montana, wed in 1976. The family moved to Williston when Russell was young. Rick and Pam also have two daughters, Lynn and Monica. Lynn lives in Bismarck, North Dakota, and is married to Cody Lindstrom, and between them they have seven adult children, four grandchildren, two daughters-in-law and a couple of the kids are in committed relationships. Monica is married to Greg Abell, and they have two children, Annabel and Emmit, and reside in Alexander, ND.

Russell and Katie welcomed a son, Jeten Liam Don Wyman, on November 19, 2010, welcomed Paisley Taylor Kay on November 10, 2011 and welcomed Maverick Russell Evans on January 5, 2017.

Jeten, Paisley and Maverick have a great grandma residing in Williston as well, Dorothy Polson.

www.ingramcontent.com/pod-product-compliance
Lightning Source LLC
LaVergne TN
LVHW061624070526
838199LV00070B/6573